Now y...
alto sax...
specially recorded arrangements

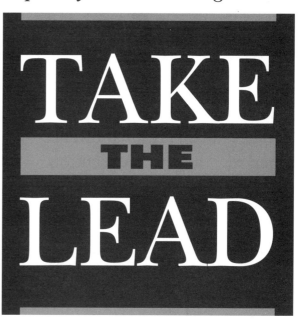

TAKE THE LEAD

alto saxophone

IMP
International MUSIC Publications

International Music Publications Limited
Griffin House 161 Hammersmith Road London W6 8BS England

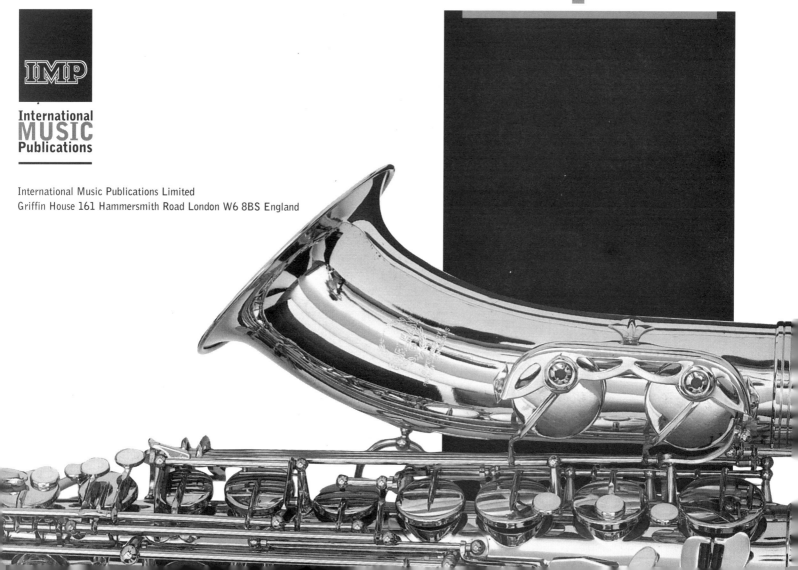

Series Editor: Sadie Cook

Editorial, production and recording: Artemis Music Limited
Design and production: Space DPS Limited

Published 1999

International MUSIC Publications

International Music Publications Limited

England:	Griffin House 161 Hammersmith Road London W6 8BS	**Italy:**	Via Campania 12 20098 San Giuliano Milanese Milano
Germany:	Marstallstr. 8 D-80539 München	**Spain:**	Magallanes 25 28015 Madrid
Denmark:	Danmusik Vognmagergade 7 DK1120 Copenhagen K	**France:**	20 Rue de la Ville-l'Eveque 75008 Paris

Carisch

alto saxophone

TAKE THE LEAD

In the Book...

On the CD...

Birdland

Demonstration

Backing

Music by
Josef Zawinul

Desafinado

Demonstration   Backing

Words by Newton Ferriera de Mendonca
Music by Antonio Carlos Jobim

Moderate Bossa Nova

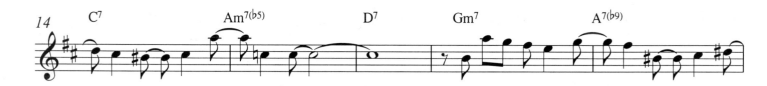

Don't Get Around Much Anymore

Demonstration   Backing

Music by Duke Ellington

Demonstration   Backing

Fascinating Rhythm

Music and Lyrics by
George Gershwin and Ira Gershwin

Moderate Swing

Misty

Music by Erroll Garner

My Funny Valentine

Music by Richard Rodgers

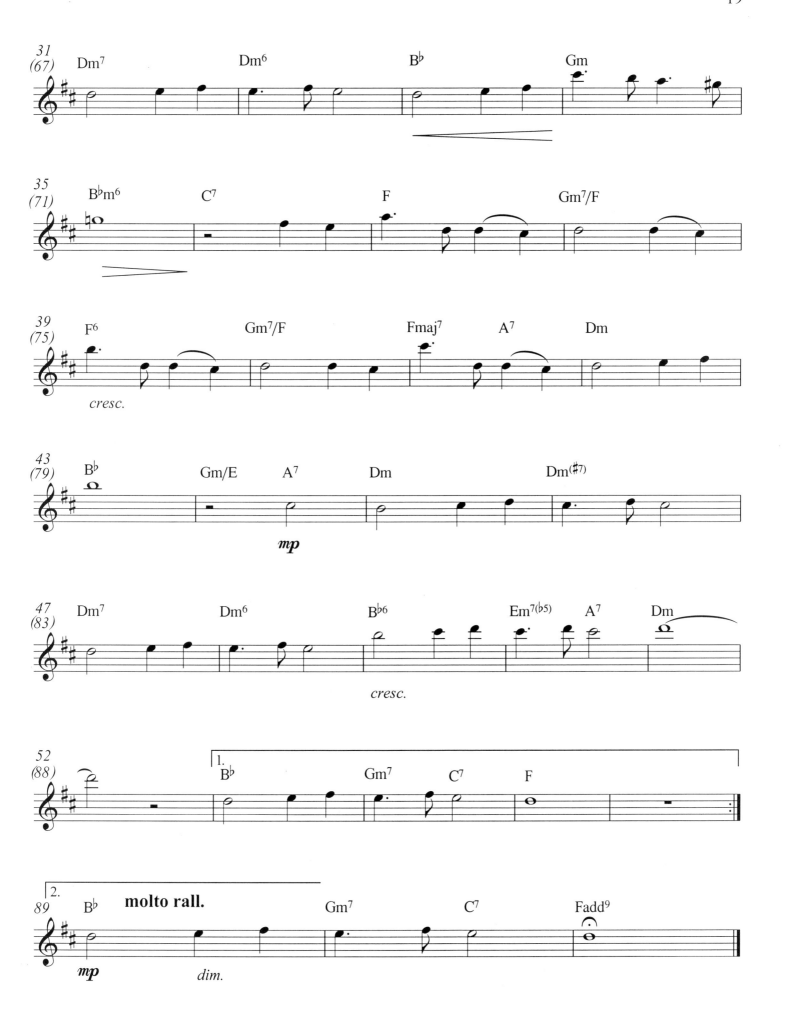

20

Demonstration   Backing

One O'Clock Jump

Music by Count Basie

Bright Swing

Summertime

Music and Lyrics by George Gershwin,
Du Bose and Dorothy Heyward and Ira Gershwin

Reproduced and printed by
Halstan & Co. Ltd., Amersham, Bucks., England

2/02

You can be the featured soloist with
TAKE THE LEAD

Now you can be the feature clarinet soloist on eight specially recorded arrangements

TAKE THE LEAD

clarinet

MOVIE HITS

FEATURES
- Full backings to play along with
- Full demonstration tracks to help you learn the songs
- Carefully selected and edited arrangements
- Chord symbols in concert pitch

Collect these titles, each with demonstration and full backing tracks on CD.

90s Hits	Movie Hits	TV Themes	Christmas Songs	The Blues Brother
The Air That I Breathe (Simply Red)	Because You Loved Me (Up Close And Personal)	Coronation Street	The Christmas Song (Chestnuts Roasting On An Open Fire)	She Caught The Katy And Left Me A Mule To Ride
Angels (Robbie Williams)	Blue Monday (The Wedding Singer)	I'll Be There For You (theme from *Friends*)	Frosty The Snowman	Gimme Some Lovin'
How Do I Live (LeAnn Rimes)	(Everything I Do) I Do It For You (Robin Hood: Prince Of Thieves)	Match Of The Day	Have Yourself A Merry Little Christmas	Shake A Tail Feather
I Don't Want To Miss A Thing (Aerosmith)	I Don't Want To Miss A Thing (Armageddon)	(Meet) The Flintstones	Little Donkey	Everybody Needs Someboc To Love
I'll Be There For You (The Rembrandts)	I Will Always Love You (The Bodyguard)	Men Behaving Badly	Rudolph The Red-Nosed Reindeer	The Old Landmark
My Heart Will Go On (Celine Dion)	Star Wars (Main Title) (Star Wars)	Peak Practice	Santa Claus Is Comin' To Town	Think
Something About The Way You Look Tonight (Elton John)	The Wind Beneath My Wings (Beaches)	The Simpsons	Sleigh Ride	Minnie The Moocher
Frozen (Madonna)	You Can Leave Your Hat On (The Full Monty)	The X-Files	Winter Wonderland	Sweet Home Chicago
Order ref: 6725A – Flute	Order ref: 6908A – Flute	Order ref: 7003A – Flute	Order ref: 7022A – Flute	Order ref: 7079A - Flute
Order ref: 6726A – Clarinet	Order ref: 6909A – Clarinet	Order ref: 7004A – Clarinet	Order ref: 7023A – Clarinet	Order ref: 7080A - Clarinet
Order ref: 6727A – Alto Saxophone	Order ref: 6910A – Alto Saxophone	Order ref: 7005A – Alto Saxophone	Order ref: 7024A – Alto Saxophone	Order ref: 7081A - Alto Saxophone
Order ref: 6728A – Violin	Order ref: 6911A –Tenor Saxophone	Order ref: 7006A – Violin	Order ref: 7025A – Violin	Order ref: 7082A - Tenor Saxophon
	Order ref: 6912A – Violin		Order ref: 7026A – Piano	Order ref: 7083A - Trumpet
			Order ref: 7027A – Drums	Order ref: 7084A - Violin